P9-DMV-731

taylor lautner

Josie Rusher

introduction

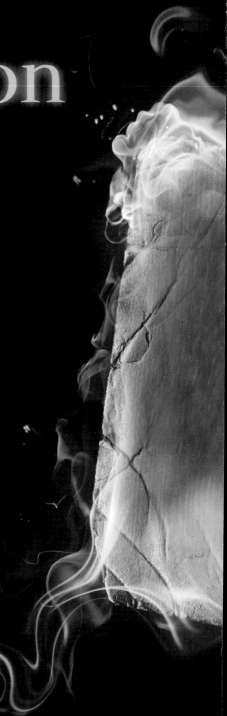

As the *Twilight* film series continues to grip fans around the globe, it's been bringing to our attention some seriously hot talent. Although his character was an average teenage boy in *Twilight*, Taylor Lautner went through an amazing transformation for the following films. From kid-next-door to werewolf – from boy to smoking-hot leading man – our Taylor is a multi-talented actor who's about to set the world on fire.

It seems impossible to imagine, but Taylor never thought he wanted to be an actor when he was young. His karate instructor thought he'd be great on screen, so encouraged him – and just look where he is now!

But don't imagine that all the stardom has gone to his head – this is one boy with his feet firmly on the ground. Everyone who worked with him on the *Twilight* series said he was sweet, polite and grateful, and worked hard. Though that could have been because he had his dad around – the whole time! But really, it's just because he's such a great, respectful sweetie.

But what's his idea of the perfect date? How would he describe himself in three words? Did he get along with all his co-stars on the *New Moon* and *Eclipse* sets? Read on for all this delicious gossip, plus some exclusive bits from behind the scenes of the movie series that pits man against vampire against werewolf. Hot stuff!

Factfile:
Meet Taylor

Full name: Taylor Daniel Lautner

Birthday: 11 February, 1992

Birthplace: Grand Rapids, Michigan

Current location: Los Angeles, California

Height: 5′ 10½″

Eye colour: brown

Hair colour: brown

Family: mum Deborah, dad Dan and younger sister Makena

School: He was attending Valencia High School in California, but recently started taking college classes in his own time instead.

Pets: Taylor loves animals – he has a pet Maltese named Roxie.

Celeb friends: He is good friends with all his *Twilight* co-stars, especially Kristen Stewart and Nikki Reed. He's also friends with Gishel Rafael, Alyson Stoner and Taylor Dooley.

Ancestry: French, Dutch, German and Native American (specifically Ottawa and Potawatomi)

Sports: Taylor's a sports fanatic. He enjoys playing American football, baseball and basketball, and he supports college teams, the Texas Longhorns and the Michigan Wolverines.

Favourite colour: baby blue

Favourite food: Mexican, Chinese, steak

Favourite ice cream flavour: cake batter

Favourite actors: Denzel Washington, Brad Pitt, Matt Damon

Favourite actresses: Jessica Alba, Megan Fox

Favourite movie: He really likes action drama movies, like *The Dark Knight*, *Iron Man*, and the Bourne series, but has recently started watching horror films, too: 'My friends just introduced me to how great horror movies can be. I really liked *The Hitcher*, and *Gothika* gave me nightmares!'

Favourite superhero: Taylor says 'I love watching the *Spider-Man* movies. Although he's probably not my favourite superhero, I love watching the movies. As for a super power, I like x-ray vision, like Superman, who can see right through things. I think that's pretty cool.'

Favourite TV shows: *American Idol* and *So You Think You Can Dance*

Favourite bands: Taylor is really open minded about music. He says he loves everything, but always tries to keep up with the top ten on iTunes.

Secret talent: He's creative. He made up a music video for Timbaland featuring OneRepublic's song 'Apologize'.

Other secret talent: Taylor is a kick-ass martial artist! By the age of 12, he had three Junior World Championships under his karate 'black belt'.

Himself in three words: 'Friendly, outgoing, energetic'

Really wants to learn: to skateboard

On Saturday nights: Taylor likes to play video games on the PS2 at his friends' houses. He loves being busy, but given his schedule these days, he looks forward to days when he can just chill out and relax.

Fun fact: He can't stop tapping his foot when he's nervous.

If he weren't an actor: 'I'd probably still be playing sports. I did football and baseball my whole life. I definitely like writing too and maybe I'd be trying to be getting in the directing field, but I'm glad that I'm an actor.'

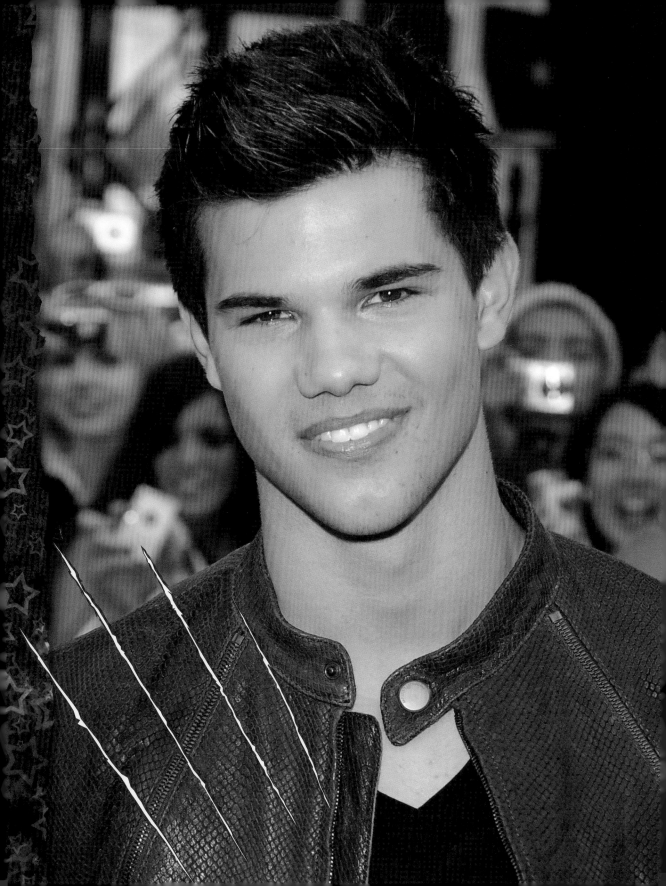

chapter 1

meet taylor

Born on 11 February, 1992 in Grand Rapids,
Michigan, Taylor Lautner seemed to be destined
to hit the big time. At just six years old, he
started studying karate at Fabiano's Karate
School and was winning tournaments within
a year. He was ranked world number one by
age eleven. Super talented!

Background

But Taylor says he owes his success in showbiz to someone
other than himself. 'My karate instructor was involved in
show business and he kind of took me into the business,'
says Taylor. 'Whenever I would come out to LA to train for
karate with him, I would go out on auditions, and eventually I realised that I liked acting more. So I gave up karate for
acting, and now I'm very glad I made that choice.' So are we!

After a while, the family were getting tired of all the
travelling to and from auditions. So his parents – who
were totally supportive of their son's dream – moved the
family to Los Angeles, so that Taylor could audition on a
full-time basis.

Taylor was sad to leave friends and family behind. 'It was a very, very hard decision,' he says. 'Our family and friends did not want us to go. But our choices were: We could stay in Michigan and I could give up acting. (I would have had to because it would have been crazy to continually fly out from Michigan to California each time there was an audition!) Or we could move to California and I could continue to act. I told my parents I didn't want to give up acting. And after weighing the good with bad, they agreed to move. Of course, we were all sad that our house was gone in Michigan. But it turned out for the best because we're having a lot of fun in California now!'

And boy, how it worked out! The young karate expert managed to win roles on TV shows like *The Bernie Mac Show* and *The Nick & Jessica Variety Hour*, as well as doing voiceovers on cartoons like *What's New, Scooby-Doo?* and *Charlie Brown*.

'I gave up karate for acting, and now I'm very glad I made that choice.'

TAYLOR

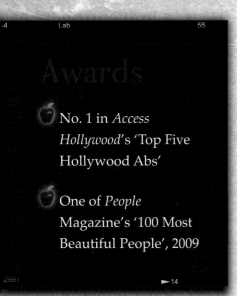

Awards

- No. 1 in *Access Hollywood*'s 'Top Five Hollywood Abs'

- One of *People* Magazine's '100 Most Beautiful People', 2009

But his big break came when he was 13, and he won the role of Shark Boy in the film *The Adventures of Sharkboy and Lavagirl 3-D*. He says that filming the movie was one of the most enjoyable experiences of his life, and within months he had another role lined up, this time in *Cheaper by the Dozen 2*.

So, when the role of the friendly, protective boy-next-door who's in love with Bella – and also happens to be a werewolf – came up in *Twilight*, Taylor just knew the part was meant to be his. It was the most excited Taylor's ever been to win a role – but he had no way of knowing how big *Twilight* was going to be – or what was in store for him next!

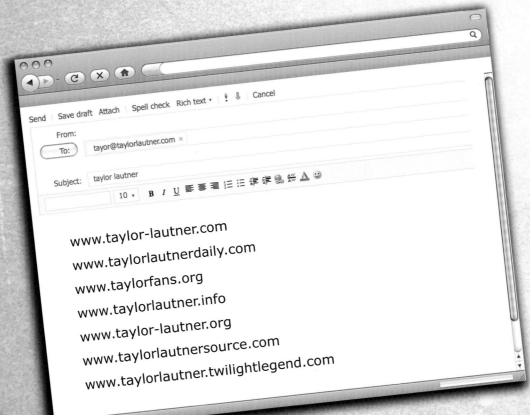

Send | Save draft | Attach | Spell check | Rich text ▾ | ! ⬇ | Cancel

From:

To: tayor@taylorlautner.com ✕

Subject: taylor lautner

10 ▾ **B** *I* U̲

www.taylor-lautner.com

www.taylorlautnerdaily.com

www.taylorfans.org

www.taylorlautner.info

www.taylor-lautner.org

www.taylorlautnersource.com

www.taylorlautner.twilightlegend.com

55
Frame
54

32991
▶ 14

54 Lab 55

32991 ▶ 14

PhotoFreak

55

54 Shutter

55

32991 ▶ 14

32991

▶ 14

What's in a name?

Taylor Lautner is real-life best buds with *Adventures of Sharkboy and Lavagirl* co-stars Taylor Dooley and Cayden Boyd. In fact, he has a lot in common with Taylor Dooley: they have the same first name; he was born in Grand Rapids, Michigan, and she was born in Grosse Point, Michigan; they both celebrate their birthdays in February, though a year apart (hers is on the 26th in 1993); their mothers share the same name and they live minutes apart in their new homes in Los Angeles!

TAYLOR ON HIS FAVOURITE BOOK

'The *Twilight* series! I actually wasn't much of a book reader at all before the *Twilight* series. They just draw you in and people love them. They're terrific books.'

Fact or fiction?

Although a lot of people seem to think Taylor is a hip-hop street dancer, that's actually not true! 'That's on some of my biographies. I need to get that off because I did it when I was ten years old and I did it for about six months and I was done with it,' he says.

Acting talent and beyond

'I also love directing and editing and filming things. When I was in public high school I took a video production class, and we got to make music videos, homemade movies. I love that too, the whole process, writing it, putting it in storyboards, then filming it and editing it and then just having the final product is really cool!'

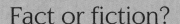

TAYLOR ON HIS DANCING

'I can't dance at all, so I need to clear that up!'

chapter 2

twilight

When Bella Swan's mother remarries, she
decides to leave Phoenix, Arizona to go and
live with her father in the rainy little town of
Forks in Washington. At school, Bella meets the
mysteriously attractive Edward Cullen, who
at first acts like he hates her, but after rescuing
her from a late-night encounter with some
drunken hooligans, professes he can't stay away
from her any longer and a rather unusual love
affair begins. It's unusual because Edward has
superhuman speed and strength, his skin glitters
like diamonds in the sunlight, he's been
a vampire since 1918 and despite being attracted
to Bella, he also thirsts for her blood.

Luckily for Bella, Edward's family are vegetarian
vampires – only feeding on animals, not humans.
But he must still fight his thirst for her.

Although Bella meets and is welcomed by Edward's family (for the most part), when unexpected vampire visitors realise there is a human among the Cullen coven they set out to kill Bella. The film culminates in a fight to save Bella's life. But can the forbidden love between a vampire and a mortal ever succeed?

To complicate matters, Bella also attracts the attentions of sweet, boy-next-door, Jacob – a childhood friend – who has Bella's best interests at heart, and doesn't trust the Cullens at all …

All the action takes place against the backdrop of an American high school, with all the usual issues you'd expect to find there while the students prepare for their prom.

TAYLOR ON HIS COSTUME FOR *TWILIGHT*

'Everyone else got the cool costumes and the makeup, the pale skin and the coloured contacts. All I got was this long black wig that reached halfway down my back. I hated it. It was the hottest, itchiest, most uncomfortable thing I've ever worn. I couldn't wait to get it off at the end of the day'

On being Jacob

Taylor had some work to do for the first film. As his character Jacob is a Native American of the Quileute tribe, Taylor hit the books, studying all the Quileute legends and myths. He even met some tribe members in person.

'When we went to Portland to film, I was able to meet with about ten Quileute tribal members. I got to talk to them and what I really learned is that they're not much different than me, and that was unexpected. I'd have to say the biggest surprise for me was learning that the kids are just like me. Their hobbies are football and "checking out girls on the beach"!

'One thing the Quilèute do that I noticed is they don't need to be told what to do. If the trash is getting full, they empty it out. They're always helping each other. They're always there for each other. So I just wanted to make sure I could bring that part of Jacob alive,' he says.

Taylor loves the contrast between the Native American side and the werewolf side of Jacob: 'His Native American side is very friendly and outgoing. He loves Bella and is very loyal to Bella and his dad. But on the werewolf side, he's fierce and attacking, with a huge temper. So there's a lot of stress and things going on inside him as he's trying to keep his temper to himself.'

Taylor also had to learn how to push his onscreen dad's wheelchair, to make it look totally natural, as well as get his driving licence, so he could drive Jacob's truck.

'I'm very similar to Jacob – I think Jacob and I are very outgoing and friendly. I'm really outgoing and crazy and just love to have fun, so I'm like that part of Jacob. Now, the other side, I'm totally opposite. When Jacob turns into a werewolf he's grumpy and fierce and I'm not like that, but I like playing that because I like to play characters that are not like me. It's a lot of fun to do!'

The Quileute tribe

Both Jacob and his dad Billy are members of the Quileute Tribe, one of the most ancient Native American tribes that still exists, and just like in the *Twilight* saga, some of their members live in Forks.

With their own people, language, songs, dances and even their own games, the Quileute tribe is definitely very different from most normal American families! In fact, it may be suitable that they are seen as also being werewolves in *Twilight* as the Quileute tribe were seen by the British, Spanish and Dutch settlers in America as one of the toughest Indian tribes around, as the Quileute used to capture entire ships full of people and keep those onboard as slaves!

When preparing to play Jacob Black, Taylor went to spend time with the Quileute tribe. He was impressed by their kindness and it was seeing that which made Taylor decide to portray Jacob as kind and gentle towards Bella.

Kristen Stewart on Taylor

'I love Taylor.
Taylor went through the
most amazing transformation.'

'With the first movie, and the first book, you don't really know much. You just know that Jacob is this really happy-go-lucky guy, who is just in love with Bella'

Favourite scene

'My favourite scene is the ballet studio, after James has bitten Bella, and Edward has sucked the poison to get the venom out of her, and he can't stop, and Carlisle is like "Edward, you're killing her, you need to stop," and he can't. He goes through these flashbacks remembering and thinking about her and what she means and he eventually stops. That's my favourite moment in the film.'

TAYLOR ON *TWILIGHT*

'I was just so excited to be a part of the movie. It's got all the romance that the girls love, plus there's great action and awesome fight scenes'

What about behind the scenes?

At just 16, Taylor was the youngest cast member in *Twilight*, so he was a little nervous on set at first. But everyone was so super nice, he found them easy to relate to, which put him right at ease.

'The cast really had great chemistry and we all hung out. We're all really good friends now, so that's really cool.' KStew, RPattz and Jackson Rathbone are all established musicians, so the cast did a lot of very cool hanging out backstage. How awesome!

Twihards

TAYLOR

'*Twilight* fans are everywhere. You're just walking down the street, or at a premiere – everywhere there are *Twilight* fans!'

Taylor hadn't heard of *Twilight* before he got the role of Jacob – but he went online to check it out, and was overwhelmed with the huge fanbase that the book series already had. 'I checked out the fan sites like twilightlexicon.com and twilightmoms.com, and it's crazy,' he says.

'Then, at my school, girls were reading it left and right. In my chemistry class, I looked to my left and a girl was reading *Twilight*, then in another class a girl was reading *New Moon*! It was pretty hilarious. I even had a substitute teacher once who said "I heard you're going to be in *Twilight* – that's my favourite book!"'

But it didn't take Taylor long to become bitten by the *Twilight* bug – he bought the books, started reading and soon he couldn't stop turning the pages. Taylor has confessed to being 'not much of a reader', but says the *Twilight* books are his favourite. Sounds like a dedicated Twihard to me!

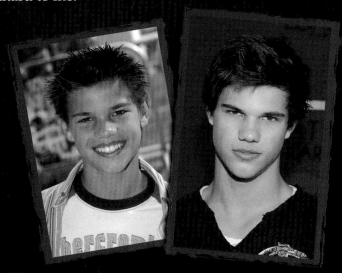

Twilight's incredible fanbase continues to surprise Taylor though: 'It's still weird to see shirts that say "Team Taylor" on them. It's very surprising, but at the same time it's not, because the fans behind it are extraordinary. We've had the criers, the hyperventilators, the shakers. It's something I've never experienced and probably never will again!'

'One of the other weirdest fan things is somebody sent me a link and said, "What is this?" And it was a picture of women's underwear being sold online with "Taylor" written on it. So it was kind of weird to have women's underwear with my name imprinted on the front.'

KEVIN JONAS

'I just recently saw *Twilight* – I was blown away'

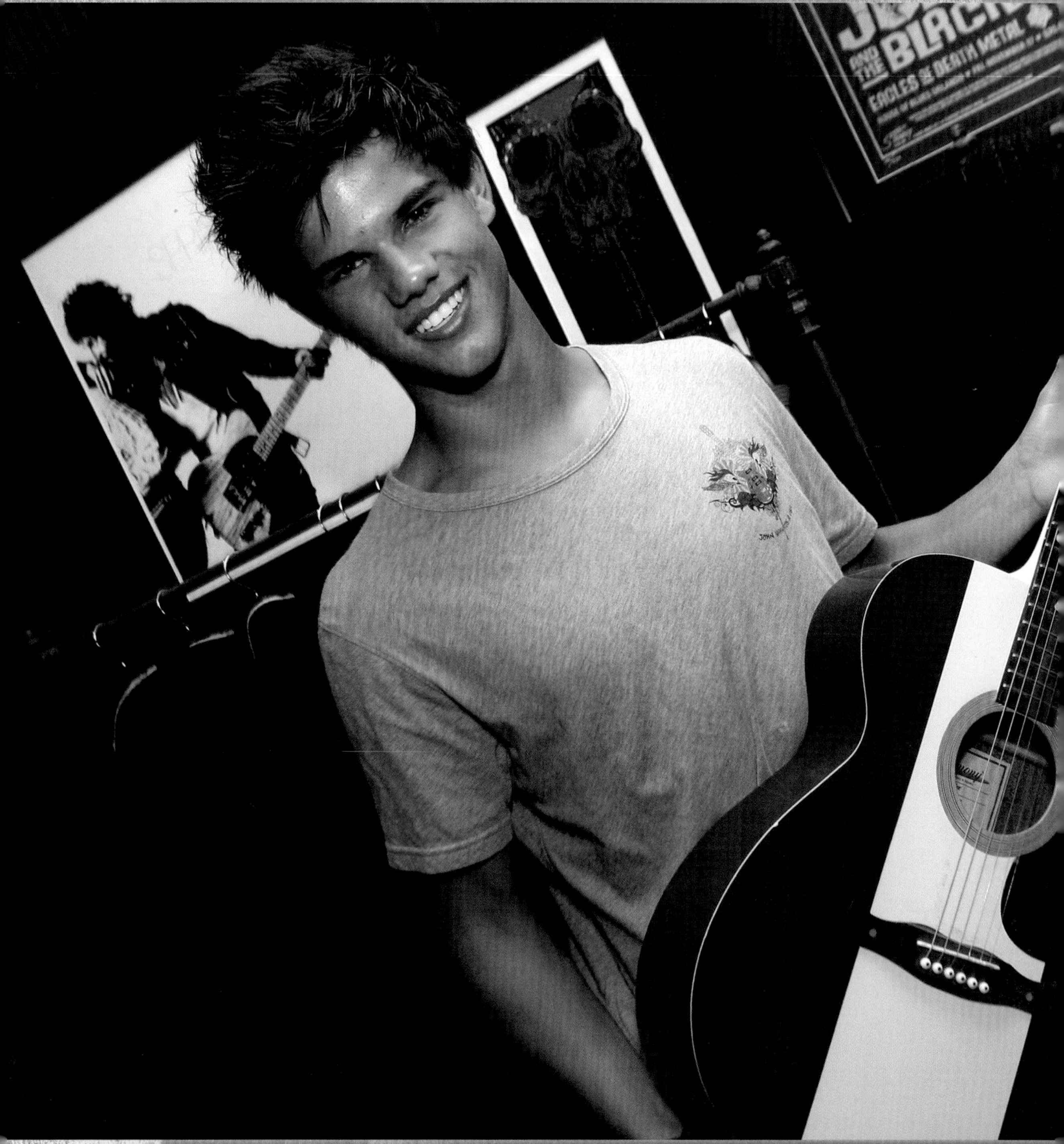
EAGLES OF DEATH METAL

Twilight trivia

🍎 It took 36 hours to turn Nikki Reed's naturally brunette hair to blonde.

🍎 The movie was shot in 48 days.

🍎 The script was finished in six weeks.

🍎 All of the actors playing the Cullens wear topaz-coloured contacts.

🍎 Robert Pattinson performed two songs in the movie, but only one of these songs, 'Never Think', appears on the soundtrack. His other song, 'Let Me Sign', is a bonus track.

🍎 At a midnight screening of *Twilight* in Texas, a guy dropped to his knee with a ring as the credits rolled. To the delight of the screaming crowd, he asked his girlfriend if theirs might be as enduring and unconditional a love as the one shared by Edward and Bella.

chapter 3

new moon

KRISTEN STEWART ON *NEW MOON*

'It's a movie about ultimate devotion being ripped from you and thinking that your entire world that you've established is wrong. And then trying to get it back and realising that it's all OK. And vampires, werewolves, too, so that makes it even more exciting. Robert Pattinson is just so cute. So is Taylor Lautner. That's what I would tell someone who doesn't know about the movie yet!'

So, what happens?

After Bella recovers from the vampire attack that almost killed her in *Twilight*, she celebrates her birthday with Edward and his family. When a paper cut draws blood, Bella is nearly attacked by Edward's brother Jasper, the newest member of the family who is still adapting to the 'vegetarian' vampire lifestyle.

To protect Bella, Edward ends the relationship and his family leaves Forks. Broken-hearted, Bella loses the motivation to do anything with her life. She resorts to reckless pursuits like motorbiking (finding that adrenaline makes her hallucinate about Edward), and she also grows closer to childhood friend Jacob Black, who has transformed into quite a hunk. She is also having constant nightmares in which Edward keeps appearing.

Bella is being hunted by evil vampire Victoria, and it is up to Jacob – a werewolf – and the rest of the Quileute Indian werewolves to protect Bella. In the meantime, Edward is distraught at the prospect of eternity without Bella and leaves for Italy, hoping to persuade the Volturi – a powerful vampire coven that impose the laws of the vampire world – to kill him. Edward's sister Alice and Bella rush to Italy to try to change Edward's mind, but will they make it in time – and can Bella choose between vampire and werewolf, now her loyalties have been tested to the limit?

What about behind the scenes?

Although Taylor is undoubtedly the screen hero in *New Moon*, it was touch and go whether he'd be given the part of Jacob in the movie! In the books, Jacob undergoes a considerable transformation between *Twilight* and *New Moon*, and Taylor was only sixteen when they were shooting, and pretty slight. So, when *Twilight* filming had ended, there were rumours the studio were looking for a new actor to play Jacob in *New Moon* – a bigger, beefier version of Taylor.

Everyone – from the Twihards who had fallen in love with him, to his co-stars who had adopted him as their little brother – was devastated. But Taylor wasn't deterred – he decided to audition for the part again, and do whatever it took to get it.

From the day that they finished shooting *Twilight*, Taylor hooked up with a personal trainer and hit the gym – sometimes two or three times a day – and ate lots of protein to make sure he bulked up enough to bring the new Jacob Black to the screen. 'I knew it was a necessity for the character,' he says.

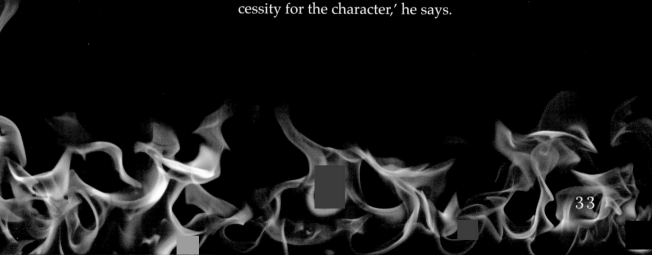

And it worked – with 30 pounds of new muscle packed on his martial-art-toned bod, Taylor won the part of Jacob in *New Moon*, and everyone heaved a sigh of relief. His cast members were over the moon – and also really impressed with his dedication to the part.

Co-stars Nikki Read and Kristen Stewart – who have grown to be like big sisters to Taylor – couldn't have been happier to have him back. 'I'm so glad they didn't have to find somebody else; we already had him!' says KStew.

But winning the role was only the beginning of the hard work. For his role as a werewolf, Taylor and the rest of the wolf pack had to shoot most of their scenes practically naked! 'The most intense scene in *New Moon* for me was when Jacob basically has to break up with Bella, because he realises he's too much for her to handle,' he says.

PETER FACINELLI – WHO PLAYS
CARLISLE CULLEN – JOKES:

'He scares me now.
He's gotten really big, and if I
saw him in a back alley, I'd probably run!'

'Jacob's doing it for her, he's not doing it for himself. But the thing that made it so intense is that I was shirtless, all I was wearing was shorts, it was thirty-five degrees Fahrenheit (two degrees Celsius), and they were pouring rain on me from a rain tower – ice-cold water, it was horrible! We couldn't look like we were cold either – you know, we're werewolves, we're hot!' You're telling us, Taylor – phew!

Having spent so much time together, Taylor, Kristen and Rob have developed great chemistry, which you can see on screen. But Taylor and KStew spent so much time together the tabloids soon forgot about her and Rob – and started gossiping about Bella and the werewolf! But Taylor has stated that he's single, and Kristen is still with her long-term boyfriend, so fear not, ladies – Taylor's still looking!

Q. Would Taylor be vampire

A. 'Definitely I'd have to go with the werewo

the

new

The wolf pack

Chaske Spencer, Bronson Pelletier, Alex Meraz, Kiowa Gordon and Tyson Houseman join Taylor Lautner in the film's La Push wolf pack. All the wolves are of Native American or First Nations descent, hailing from the Lakota (Sioux), Cree-Metis, Purepecha (Tarasco), Hualapai and Cree nations. This is one hot pack!

ilight saga

moon

(

20.09

or werewolf in real life?
– the pack! Sticking with the pack, baby!'

Werewolves

Jacob's transformation into a fully-grown werewolf is possibly the most important event in *New Moon*. The werewolves of the Quileute tribe are an ancient clan and have an uneasy relationship with the Cullen family. Here is some more information about the hairiest and scariest creatures in the *Twilight* series.

Werewolves throughout history

Many in Europe believe that the myth of werewolves began to explain mysterious or gruesome deaths of people in forests. Each country in Europe used to have its own distinct beliefs about werewolves. In Armenia, it was believed that women who committed deadly sins would be condemned to becoming a wolf for seven years. Also, in 11th Century Belarus, the people believed their own Prince Usiaslau of Polatsk was a werewolf, and would transform at night to wander the towns. Possibly the most famous werewolf story however, is the French story of the 'Beast of Gévaudan', which was believed to have killed over 80 people.

The Native Americans however, have their own beliefs about werewolves, calling them 'Skin-walkers'. A skin-walker was believed to be someone with the ability to 'steal the skin' of any animal and human they wanted and transform. The Quileute tribe in *Twilight* also reveal that they are not in fact 'werewolves' but shape-shifters who take the form of wolves.

Werewolves in film

Though Taylor might be playing the coolest werewolf ever seen on the big screen, he definitely isn't the first! That honour belongs to actors in the 1913 silent film *The Werewolf*, which is so old it is thought that all copies of the film are now lost. This was followed by the famous classic of 1941 *The Wolf Man* with the werewolf played by Lon Chaney Jnr., and the film was so successful it produced four more sequels!

In 1981, the first modern horror-film featuring were-wolves was made with *The Howling*, about a group of humans who find themselves trapped in a colony full of werewolves. Recently werewolves have been seen at war with vampires just like in the *Twilight* series in *The Underworld* films and *Van Helsing*. *New Moon*, however, won't be the only film featuring werewolves we'll hear about, as 2010 will mark the release of a remake of *The Wolf Man* film.

TAYLOR ON JACOB

'The bummer is, when he becomes a wolf, that's not actually me. When he does the cool fight scenes, he's transformed into CGI'

A typical day on set

'I have very early wake-up calls. I'm usually waking up at four-thirty or five, and we don't usually finish until about five or six at night. But we usually go out after, just explore the restaurants in town. It's been a lot of fun so far.'

Twihards

'I was in my hometown in Michigan and thought it would be fun to go to the *Breaking Dawn* release party. I was there until 2am, hanging out and signing books. It was a good time! There were over 1000 fans, and it was a nice surprise for them,' says Taylor.

TAYLOR ON TWIHARDS

'Fans are the driving force behind this thing.'

Favourite scene

'It's so hard to choose. I really enjoy the stunts so I had a lot of fun doing the dirt bike sequences. I got to hop on the bike and go really fast and come to a skidding stop. It's really cool. And I also like a lot of the more serious scenes, the pivotal scenes in the movie, like Jacob and Bella's breakup scene, which is the first time Bella sees Jacob after he has transformed into a wolf. And it's really emotional. I felt bad for Jacob just reading the books, but now that I'm actually living this character, I feel so bad for the guy! It's really sad.'

TAYLOR ON *NEW MOON*

'I was in the gym every single day, seven days a week, two hours a day, eating as much as I possibly could. It gets nerve-wracking. For the most part, I'm just really excited. Jacob's character becomes very cool and has a lot more depth in the rest of the series. I'm definitely Team Jacob.'

Factfile:

Meet Kristen

Feisty tomboy Kristen Stewart – who had only really starred in indie flicks until *Twilight* came along – was totally blown away by the success of the franchise, and the reaction of the fans to her portrayal of Bella Swan. But when asked if the fame has changed her, she's adamant that it hasn't. 'It didn't change me. To put your heart and soul into something for years of your life and have it actually affect people is probably the most satisfying, and that is a completely ineffective word to describe how satisfying it is,' she says.

Full name: Kristen Jaymes Stewart

Birthday: 9 April, 1990. Kristen turned 18 while filming the movie and was rewarded with a birthday cake – and a full night of shooting. Aw!

Birthplace: Los Angeles, California, USA

Nicknames: Kris, KStew

Height: 5' 6"

Eye colour: green – she wears brown contacts for filming to match Bella's eye colour

Hair colour: brown – she wore hair pieces for filming so they didn't have to waste time doing her hair

Relationship status: has a steady boy-friend, Michael Angarano

Favourite films: American Beauty, The Shining, ET, Spaceballs

Favourite authors: Charles Bukowski, Kurt Vonnegut Jr

Role model: her grandma, 'For her strength and resilience'

Hobbies and interests: travelling, surfing, writing (went through a poetry phase, and at one point wanted to write a novel or screenplay)

43

Factfile:

Meet Robert

Hunky werewolf Taylor is definitely the heart-throb of *New Moon*, but he's got hot competition from moody, smouldering vampire Edward Cullen – played by Brit Robert Pattinson. Check out Rob's essential facts.

Full name: Robert Thomas Pattinson

Date of birth: 13 May, 1986

Place of birth: London, England

Current location: Rents an apartment in LA, stays at his parents' pad in London and spends time in Vancouver filming

Nicknames: Rob, RPattz, Patty

Height: 6' 1"

Relationship status: single, although has been romantically linked to Paris Hilton, Natalie Portman, Rihanna, Miley Cyrus, and any other celebrity he stands within ten feet of!

Ideal night: staying in watching movies, eating fast food and playing his guitar

Fear: Rob is petrified of flying. 'I don't deal with it. I just spend the whole flight freaking out.'

Best qualities: According to best friend Sam Bradley, he's a great cook, and is just so tidy, he's a neat freak! Sounds good to us …

Accent: The *Twilight* series is his first set of films with an American accent, but Rob's had no formal training – he's just watched a lot of American TV and films!

Although RPattz was once known for playing Cedric Diggory in *Harry Potter and the Goblet of Fire*, he's now a global superstar for bringing the role of vampire Edward Cullen to life. Life for Rob couldn't have changed more – just a few years ago he was thinking of giving up acting for good. Now he barely walks the streets any more as he's always being mobbed by fans. When he does go out, he's in disguise! He says it's actually a relief to be back at work.

Twihards got a nasty shock when the story hit all the *Twilight* blogs that Rob had been replaced in *New Moon* by Zac Efron! But thankfully the stories were just an April Fool's joke. So we can all relax – RPattz isn't going anywhere!

chapter 4
style and looks

Taylor says, "the quote I love the most is Jacob's quote "Does my being half-naked bother you?" Though the answer from all of us is a massive NO! It does help that when he's not showing off his gorgeous abs, Taylor is always wearing the coolest clothes around. From the sunglasses to the shoes, Taylor has always got it right!

The look

Although in the first *Twilight* film he's best known wearing a long black wig and shapeshifting into a werewolf, off screen, Taylor rocks some pretty classic looks.

Vintage Taylor

Being rarely seen without his leather jacket, Taylor has perfected the classic vintage look, emulating the rockstar styles of Hollywood hotties like Brad Pitt and Tom Cruise. Here are a few tips for getting your boyfriend to develop the look Taylor mastered long ago!

T-shirts

Vintage t-shirts are everywhere right now so you will have no problem finding one your boyfriend likes. The most popular ones feature tattoo-style designs or images from classic rock concerts. It's a bonus if you find one with a pre-worn look to it, or maybe 70s and 80s retro colours.

Button-up shirts

This can be used as an extra layer or on its own, but a button-up shirt does look super-cool over a tee! Leave the shirt open and untucked for a casual look. To make it more interesting, try pairing a patterned shirt with a graphic tee.

One of Taylor's most treasured pieces of clothing; vintage-inspired jackets are popping up in shops everywhere so it won't be hard to find the perfect one! The most popular jackets have brand logos or sports emblems. Hoodies also look great if you add it with a leather jacket, because the hood looks great peeking out from under the jacket!

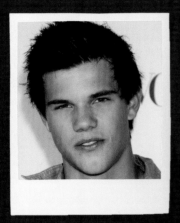

Boys need to make sure that their jeans have a roomy fit, but not too baggy or else they will look sloppy. Dark rinses are a great choice, especially if you can find some with some fraying or other subtle details.

Always choose casual, retro-looking footwear to complete the look. Skater or athletic shoes always look great, with Taylor's favourite being Vans. For an edgier look, try a pair of shoes with a crazy print, or even some suede shoes or boots if you want to be a little smarter.

And remember, the key to helping your man achieve this look is not only to choose the right items but to layer them. When creating these layers, it's ok to pair patterns like stripes with graphic images; just pick out the main colour in the graphic and use this colour in the pattern. Taylor's secret is confidence and anyone with confidence will make this look cool, hip and casual.

Clean-cut Taylor

Stepping out onto the red carpet to meet hundreds of screaming "Twihard" fans can be daunting for any actor, but wearing the right suit and knowing he looks good in it goes a long way towards making Taylor feel comfortable and at-ease with his fans. So whether it's prom time or you're going to a stylish party yourself, make sure that your date looks as cool as Taylor in his suit by following this advice.

The right fit

You never see Taylor looking uncomfortable or scruffy when he is suited up, and this is because he always makes sure it fits properly. The jacket should fit so whether it is unbuttoned or buttoned, you still can move freely in it.

The right accessories

When picking what tie to wear, remember that black ties are for the super-serious occasions. Coloured ties can be for anything, if one is worn that isn't too flashy it will add a lot to the image, but something too brightly coloured or with a crazy design will draw too much attention to it. Black is usually a good colour for a belt, unless the suit is light-coloured, when it should be brown. The belt buckle should match any other accessories, such as a watch, ear studs and cuff-links. Shoes should be comfortable and match the colour of the belt.

chapter 5

love and romance

'I look for somebody who can be
themselves. Somebody who can
just open up and be free and not
try to be somebody different'

TAYLOR ON
ROMANTIC GIFTS

'I buy roses
all the time.
Roses for
mom, roses
for everybody!
I'm a rosy
kinda guy!
I also like to
do cards.
I rarely go out
and buy cards
from a store –
I hand-make
them.'

Romance

This smoking hot werewolf has been linked with a number of lovely ladies. You might recognise some of their names – Alyson Stoner, Cassi Thomson, Sarah Hicks, Victoria Justice, Demi Lovato and Selena Gomez, to name but a few!

Taylor was seen hanging out with Selena during the filming of *New Moon*, and says he thinks the *Wizards of Waverly Place* star is a great girl. The pair were snapped by the paps going out for dinner and to get frozen yoghurt, but Taylor has stated for the record that – luckily for us – he's currently single, and looking for a lady friend!

So, what do you have to do to win this gorgeous guy's heart? 'Be yourself, open up, be crazy,' he says. Taylor believes the most important quality a girl can have is honesty. 'I look for someone honest, loyal and

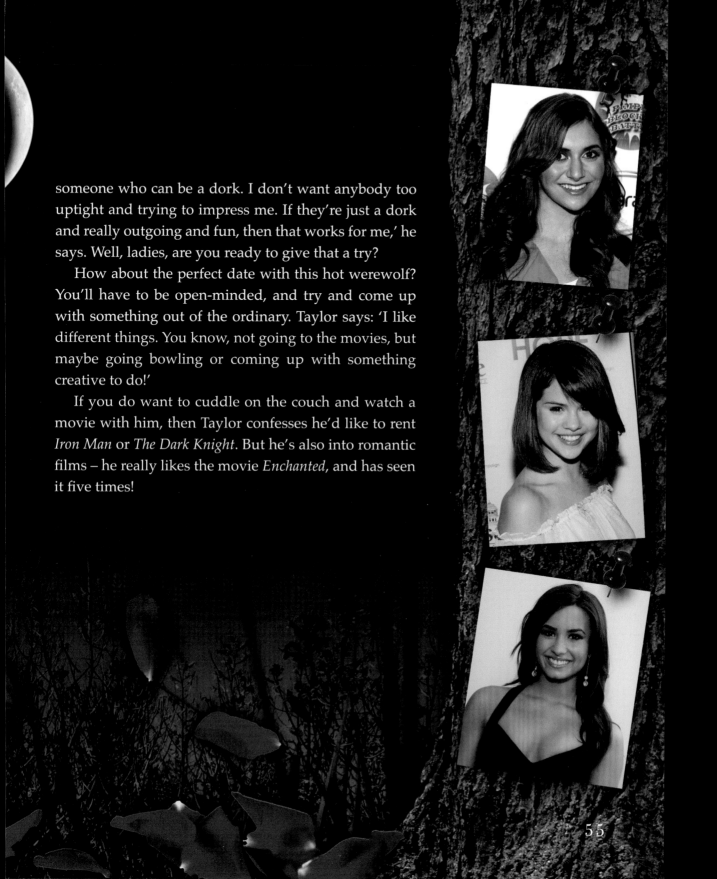

someone who can be a dork. I don't want anybody too uptight and trying to impress me. If they're just a dork and really outgoing and fun, then that works for me,' he says. Well, ladies, are you ready to give that a try?

How about the perfect date with this hot werewolf? You'll have to be open-minded, and try and come up with something out of the ordinary. Taylor says: 'I like different things. You know, not going to the movies, but maybe going bowling or coming up with something creative to do!'

If you do want to cuddle on the couch and watch a movie with him, then Taylor confesses he'd like to rent *Iron Man* or *The Dark Knight*. But he's also into romantic films – he really likes the movie *Enchanted*, and has seen it five times!

Kiss and tell!

As well as acting in movies, Taylor's also been in a music video, starring in Cassi Thomson's video for 'Caught Up In You'. Lucky old Cassi got to kiss the *Twilight* hunk! When she was asked if he was a good kisser, she said: 'Well, he's definitely not a bad one! It was more than just a peck.' We think that means yes! Go, Team Jacob!

The *Twilight* series has certainly thrust this young hunk into the spotlight, but is he ready to handle it and become a teen heart-throb? 'Oooh boy, maybe!' he says. 'Yeah, I'm looking forward to it, so we'll see what comes. I'm excited to do the *Twilight* series! It's an amazing opportunity and the fanbase behind it is incredible so I'm excited – very excited!' When Taylor and Rob were out on the town recently during filming, they got mobbed by fans, but while Rob made a run for it, Taylor turned and blew a kiss to the throngs of girls. Swoon city!

Fact or fiction?

There are rumours that Taylor is not allowed to date
until he's 28 – but these are untrue!

chapter 6

the future

With *New Moon* now finished, Taylor has a lot of
choices ahead of him. With *Eclipse* on the horizon,
the saga is far from finished but that isn't the
only thing in the pipeline, and people are already
wondering what he will do once the last film is
wrapped up and the *Twilight* "pack" break for
good. But with a cool head, and the dedication
to his roles he has already shown, Taylor doesn't
need to worry about a bright future no matter
what he decides to do.

Eclipse

Before *New Moon* had even begun filming, movie bosses were already planning the third movie in the saga – *Eclipse*! With just a tiny break after *New Moon*, the cast and crew began work on the next episode, working hard so it will be released in June 2010.

The film opens with Seattle being ravaged by a series of mysterious and gruesome killings, which Edward immediately suspects are caused by blood-hungry vampires. Meanwhile, the vampire Victoria is still determined to bring an end to Bella's life. Meanwhile, Jacob struggles to cope with his fiery love for Bella, and while she remains wholeheartedly committed to Edward, she becomes aware of Jacob's strong feelings.

The filming of *Eclipse* will also see another change of director, as Chris Weitz will make way for David Slade. Slade has previously worked on horror films, and will bring a much darker side to the third film, although if he wants to keep the shirtless scenes with Taylor that's fine with us! *Eclipse* will also introduce Australian actor Xavier Samuel playing Riley, a handsome college student who Victoria bites and changes into a blood-thirsty vampire who performs Victoria's tasks out of his love for her. The role of Victoria will also change hands with Bryce Dallas Howard, star of the *Spider Man* and *Terminator* films replacing Rachelle Lefevre. Having already bulked up for *New Moon*, Taylor will have much less of a problem adapting for his role in *Eclipse*, but he will still have the challenge of portraying a much more mature Jacob torn apart by his feelings for Bella, all while the *Twilight* universe is plunged deeper into turmoil.

Breaking from the pack

'I'd love to do a movie with Denzel Washington, or an action star such as Matt Damon or Mark Wahlberg would be really cool ... I love action films, I'd love to do an action drama.'

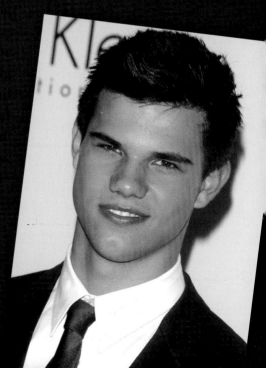

picture credits

Getty: 2, 6, 7, 8, 14, 15, 16, 18, 20, 24, 25, 26, 27, 28, 34, 39, 40, 43, 45, 46, 48, 49 (top left, top right, top centre, centre left, centre right, centre, bottom centre), 50 (top and centre), 51 (centre and bottom), 52, 55, 56, 57, 58, 60, 61, 63

Rex: 5, 10, 13, 23, 30, 32, 33, 35, 36, 38, 49 (bottom left, bottom right), 50 (bottom), 51 (top)

acknowledgements

Josie Rusher would like to thank Helia Phoenix, Amanda Harris, Helen Ewing, James Martindale, Jane Sturrock, Tim Edwards, Frank Brinkley, Viki Ottewill and Rich Carr.

Copyright © Josie Rusher 2009

The right of Josie Rusher to be identified as the author of this work has been asserted in accordance with the Copyright, Designs and Patents Act 1988.

First published in hardback in Great Britain in 2009 by Orion Books an imprint of the Orion Publishing Group Ltd

Orion House, 5 Upper St Martin's Lane London WC2H 9EA

An Hachette UK Company

10 9 8 7 6 5 4 3 2 1

All rights reserved. Apart from any use permitted under UK copyright law, this publication may only be reproduced, stored or transmitted, in any form, or by any means, with prior permission in writing of the publishers or, in the case of reprographic production, in accordance with the terms of licences issued by the Copyright Licensing Agency.

A CIP catalogue record for this book is available from the British Library.

ISBN: 978 1 4091 1528 1

Designed by Viki Ottewill

Printed in Canada

The Orion Publishing Group's policy is to use papers that are natural, renewable and recyclable and made from wood grown in sustainable forests. The logging and manufacturing processes are expected to conform to the environmental regulations of the country of origin. Every effort has been made to fulfil requirements with regard to reproducing copyright material.

The author and publisher will be glad to rectify any omissions at the earliest opportunity.

www.orionbooks.co.uk